**HEINEMANN
STATE STUDIES**

Uniquely
Michigan

Nichole Thieda

Heinemann Library
Chicago, Illinois

Designed by Heinemann Library
Photo research by Stephanie L. Miller
Printed in the United States by Lake Book
    Manufacturing, Inc.

08 07 06 05 04
10 9 8 7 6 5 4 3 2 1

**Library of Congress
Cataloging-in-Publication Data**
Thieda, Nichole, 1976-
  Uniquely Michigan / Nichole Thieda.
    v. cm. -- (Heinemann state studies)
Includes bibliographical references (p.) and index.
Contents: The Wolverine State -- State symbols -- Government -- National parks -- Business and products -- Food -- Sports -- Attractions and landmarks -- Folklore and legends -- Buildings and structures.
  ISBN 1-4034-0663-4 -- ISBN 1-4034-2681-3 (pbk.)
  1. Michigan--Juvenile literature. [1. Michigan.] I. Title. II. Series.
  F566.3.T47 2003
  977.4--dc22

                                    2003017158

Acknowledgments
The author and publishers are grateful to the following for permission to reproduce copyright material: Title page (L-R) Nichole Thieda/Heinemann Library, Nichole Thieda/Heinemann Library, Copyright 2000 by City of Grand Haven; contents page (L-R) James L. Amos/Corbis, Joseph Sohm/ChromoSohm Inc./Corbis; p. 4 Stone/Getty Images; p. 6 OneMileUp; p. 7t Ron Austing/Frank Lane Picture Agency/Corbis; p. 7b Heinemann Library; p. 8 Exhibit Museum of Natural History/The University of Michigan; p. 9t Gerlach Nature Photography/Animals Animals; p. 9b Richard Kolar/Animals Animals; p. 10 Randy Schaetzl/Geography Department/Michigan State University; p. 12 Al Goldis/AP Wide World Photos; p. 13 Dale Atkins/AP Wide World Photos; p. 14 Joseph Sohm/ChromoSohm Inc./Corbis; p. 15 Carlos Osorio/AP Wide World Photos; p. 16 John and Ann Mahan; p. 17 Conrad Zobel/Corbis; pp. 18, 19, 25, 26b, 39, 42, 43b Robert Lifson/Heinemann Library; pp. 20, 31 James L. Amos/Corbis; p. 21 Mollie J. Hoppes/The Daily News-Sun/AP Wide World Photos; p. 22t The Advertising Archive; p. 22b Reprinted with permission of Gerber Corporation; p. 23 Dennis Gottlieb/FoodPix; p. 26t Paul Conklin/PhotoEdit, Inc.; pp. 27, 29t Reuters NewMedia Inc./Corbis; p. 28 Bettmann/Corbis; p. 29b Duomo/Corbis; p. 30 AAGPBL Players Association; p. 32 maps.com/Heinemann Library; p. 33 Kit Kittle/Corbis; p. 34 Phil Schermeister/Corbis; pp. 35, 37b, 38 Nichole Thieda/Heinemann Library; pp. 37t, 41 Dennis MacDonald/Photo Edit; p. 43t Copyright 2000 by City of Grand Haven; p. 44 Layne Kennedy/Corbis; p. 45 Kimberly Saar/Heinemann Library

Cover photographs by (top, L-R) Unicorn Stock Photos, Robert Lifson/Heinemann Library, Ed Wargin/Corbis, Peter Yates/Corbis; (main) Dennis MacDonald/Photo Edit

The publisher would like to thank Charlene Rimsa for her help with the preparation of this book.

Also, special thanks to Alexandra Fix and Bernice Anne Houseward for their curriculum guidance.

Every effort has been made to contact copyright holders of any material reproduced in this book. Any omissions will be rectified in subsequent printings if notice is given to the publisher.

Some words are shown in bold, **like this.** You can find out what they mean by looking in the glossary.

Contents

The Wolverine State

There are many reasons why Michigan is a unique state. Its location in the United States is one-of-a-kind. Only in Michigan can you go south to enter Canada. It is also the only state that touches four of the five Great Lakes—Michigan, Huron, Superior, and Erie. Michigan is the only state in the mainland United States that is physically divided into two distinct parts: the Upper and Lower Peninsulas. Michigan also has the most coastline of any state in the mainland United States.

The state of Michigan has several nicknames, such as the Great Lakes State, Water Wonderland, and Lady of the Lake. But the nickname the state is probably best known by is the Wolverine State. What makes this

Many people enjoy swimming and other sports in Michigan's waters during the summer.

nickname unique is that there are no wolverines in Michigan, and there probably never were. There are several stories about how the nickname may have come about.

Some historians believe that the Native Americans living in the area that is now Michigan were frightened by the white settlers moving there. The Native Americans may have thought of the settlers as vicious "wolverines" who stole their land. Another idea is that the nickname came from a conflict with the people of the state of Ohio. During the Toledo War in 1835, there was a strip of land that both the state of Ohio and the people of the Michigan Territory called their own. Before Michigan could become a state, the argument over who owned the land had to be settled. Ohio eventually got the land, but it is thought that they may have nicknamed the people of Michigan "wolverines" because they fought so hard to keep the land for themselves.

Unique Facts About Michigan

- Almost one million boats are registered in Michigan.
- There are over 6,000 miles of trails and mountains for winter sports such as sledding, skiing, and snowmobiling.
- The world's largest weather vane stands in Montague. It is 48 feet high, 14 feet wide, and weighs 4,300 pounds.
- Michigan built the first border-to-border interstate highway in 1971. I-94 runs 205 miles from Detroit to New Buffalo.
- Michigan's Upper Peninsula is as big as Connecticut, Delaware, Massachusetts, and Rhode Island combined.
- The first traffic tunnel built between two nations was the mile-long Detroit-Windsor Tunnel under the Detroit River.

State Symbols

Each state has official state symbols. These symbols are often chosen by the state government to represent unique qualities of the state.

STATE FLAG

Michigan's state flag was **adopted** in 1911. The flag has a blue background and a **coat of arms.** The elements on the state coat of arms date from 1835. It was modeled after a coat of arms of the Hudson Bay Company, a fur-trading company in the 1600s. The Latin sayings on the coat of arms mean: "From Many, One," "I will defend," and the state motto, "If you seek a pleasant **peninsula,** look about you." Also on the coat of arms is a man with one hand raised in a greeting and a rifle in his other hand. He was added for several reasons. In the year the coat of arms was created, Michigan was involved in a struggle against Ohio for the Toledo Strip, a piece of land both states claimed as their own. There were also many people in the state who used guns to get food. The eagle on the coat of arms symbolizes the United States, and the elk and moose are **native** to Michigan.

Michigan state flag

A Different State Bird?

In Michigan, some people would like to see the Kirtland's warbler named as the state bird. This bird is currently on both the federal and state **endangered species** lists.

Others think the chickadee would be the best choice for state bird because it stays in Michigan year-round.

STATE BIRD: ROBIN

The Michigan Audobon Society recommended the robin as the state bird in 1931. However, the robin is not a symbol unique to Michigan. Connecticut and Wisconsin also chose the robin as their state birds.

STATE TREE: WHITE PINE

Michigan's state tree represents Michigan's role as a lumber provider in the 1800s. Michigan was once the leading state in logging. Millions of trees were cut down to provide wood for the needs of settlers. When the city of Chicago burned down in 1871, the white pine trees of Michigan were used to rebuild the city. There are several forests in Michigan that are home to white pine trees over 300 years old. The white pine was named Michigan's state tree in 1955.

Petoskey stone

STATE STONE: PETOSKEY STONE

The state stone is actually a **fossil.** Petoskey stones are the remains of a group of corals that lived in the Michigan area about 350 million years ago. Michigan was once covered by a salty sea where *Hexagonaria* corals lived. **Glaciers** brought the fossilized remains of these corals to the surface almost two million years ago.

Mastodon skeleton

Since then, Petoskey stones have been found along Michigan's beaches, where the movement of the water and sand has brought the stones to the surface. The Petoskey stone was named as the state stone in 1965 by the Michigan **legislature.**

STATE FOSSIL: MASTODON

The students of Slauson Middle School in Ann Arbor **campaigned** to have the **mastodon** named the state **fossil** in 2002. One of the most complete mastodon skeletons ever found was in Owosso, which is near Flint. The skeleton now stands in the University of Michigan Exhibit Museum of Natural History in Ann Arbor. Other fossils of mastodons have been found in more than 250 locations in Michigan.

STATE FLOWER: APPLE BLOSSOM

Michigan's state **legislators** named the apple blossom the state flower in 1897. Every spring, apple trees blossom with flowers that eventually become apples.

Michigan is home to about 8.5 million apple trees. Apple orchards run the length of Michigan's fruit belt, which stretches from the southwest corner of the state to Traverse City in the northwest corner. Southeast Michigan also has many apple orchards.

STATE GAME MAMMAL: WHITE-TAILED DEER

In 1997, a group of fourth grade students from Zeeland asked that the white-tailed deer be named the state game mammal. No one knows for sure the exact number of white-tailed deer in Michigan. It is estimated that there are around two million. They are found in

Dwarf lake iris

every county and are considered an important natural and **economic resource.**

STATE WILDFLOWER: DWARF LAKE IRIS

The dwarf lake iris grows only along the shores of Lakes Michigan and Huron. The plant, which has small, bright blue flowers, was discovered on Mackinac Island in 1810. However, the plant is listed on both the state and federal lists of **threatened species.** In 1998, the dwarf lake iris was designated as the state wildflower.

STATE REPTILE: PAINTED TURTLE

The painted turtle was **nominated** as the state reptile in 1995 after a group of fifth grade students in Niles discovered that Michigan did not have a state reptile. The painted turtle was accepted as the official reptile because it is the state's most common turtle. The midland painted turtle lives in the Lower Peninsula and the eastern part of the Upper Peninsula. The western painted turtle makes its home in the western part of the Upper Peninsula. It lives in Michigan's lakes and rivers. It especially likes the shallow, muddy streams where it can **burrow** and **hibernate** during the cold winters.

Painted turtle

State Fish: Brook Trout

The trout has been Michigan's state fish since 1965, but the brook trout became the official Michigan symbol in 1988. This popular fish, named the official state fish in eight states, swims in cold water streams throughout the Lower and Upper Peninsulas. Of the state's 38,000 miles of rivers and streams, only 12,500 miles are cold enough, around 50° F, to support brook trout.

State Soil: Kalkaska Soil

Kalkaska soil

Kalkaska soil is only found in Michigan. It was first identified as a soil type in 1926, and ranges from yellowish brown to black in color. The soil was named after Kalkaska County in north central Michigan. Kalkaska soil is used for growing trees such as the sugar maple and yellow birch. It is important for producing Christmas trees and specialty crops, such as potatoes and strawberries. Kalkaska soil is also used in wildlife **habitat** areas, building sites, and **recreation** areas. In 1990, the Michigan **legislature** named Kalkaska soil the state soil.

State Gemstone: Greenstone

Chlorastrolite is the full name of Michigan's state gemstone. The name means "green star stone." This stone is found in the Upper Peninsula, and was **adopted** as the state gemstone in 1972. A raw greenstone is not very pretty, but when it is polished, it has a beautiful pattern similar to a turtle shell. Greenstones were created by volcanoes that formed the western Upper Peninsula, and are thought to be about one billion years old.

STATE SONG

Michigan does not have an official state song. Michigan's House of Representatives and Senate passed a bill in 1937 that said "My Michigan" is "*an* official song of the State of Michigan." However, it is not *the* official state song. "Michigan, My Michigan" has long been considered Michigan's "unofficial" state song.

Winifred Lee Brent Lyster of Detroit wrote the **lyrics** for the first version of "Michigan, My Michigan" in 1862. Her husband, Henry, was a Civil War surgeon, and Mrs. Lyster wrote the song after the Battle of Fredericksburg. Douglas Malloch composed new lyrics in 1902.

Michigan, My Michigan

A song to thee, fair State of mine,
Michigan, my Michigan.
But greater song than this is thine,
Michigan, my Michigan.
The whisper of the towering tree,
The thunder of the **inland** sea,
United in one grand symphony
Michigan, my Michigan.

I sing a song of all the best—
Michigan, my Michigan.
I sing a State with riches blessed,
Michigan, my Michigan.
Thy mines unmask a hidden store,
But richer thy historic lore,
More great the love thy builders bore,
Michigan, my Michigan.

Glow fair the bosom of thy lakes,
Michigan, my Michigan.
What melody each river makes,
Michigan, my Michigan.
As to thy lakes thy rivers tend,
Thy exiled ones still to thee send
Devotion that shall never end,
Michigan, my Michigan.

Rich in the wealth that makes a State,
Michigan, my Michigan.
Great in the things that make men great,
Michigan, my Michigan.
Eager the voice that sounds thy claim
Under the golden roll of Fame
Willing the hand that writes the name
Of Michigan, my Michigan.

Government

On January 26, 1837, Michigan became the 26th state of the United States. The state's leaders modeled the state government after the U.S. government. Michigan's government has three branches: **executive, legislative,** and **judicial.**

EXECUTIVE BRANCH

The executive branch of Michigan's government carries out the laws. The chief executive is the governor. The governor can serve a maximum of eight years. Voters also elect the **lieutenant governor,** the secretary of state, the **attorney general,** and the state treasurer. These positions are also limited to eight years in office.

LEGISLATIVE BRANCH

The legislative branch of Michigan makes the state laws. It is made up of the state house of representatives and the state senate.

The House of Representatives has 110 members who are elected on even-numbered years. They serve two years in office, and can serve three terms, or six years total. Each **legislator** represents a **district** in the state.

During their two years in office, representatives will introduce and vote on over 4,000 bills. Only 600 to 800 of these bills will become laws.

The Senate has 38 members who are elected at the same time as the governor. Senators serve four-year terms and are limited to two terms. Terms for senators begin on January 1, after the November general election.

JUDICIAL BRANCH

Michigan's judicial branch **interprets** and applies the state's laws in real-life situations. There are hundreds of courthouses that serve different needs in the state. Michigan's court system includes circuit courts, probate courts, a court of appeals, and the state supreme court.

The Michigan Supreme Court is the highest court in the state. Seven justices serve on the supreme court. There is one chief justice and six associate justices. The justices are elected to serve eight-year terms, and every two years, one justice is selected to serve as the chief justice.

From left to right: Michigan Supreme Court justices Robert Young Jr., Clifford Taylor, Michael Cavanagh, Elizabeth Weaver, Marilyn Kelly, Maura Corrigan, and Stephen Markman.

STATE CAPITOL

Lansing was named the **capital** city of Michigan in 1847, and the **capitol** building was built in 1879. The building was patterned after the U.S. Capitol in Washington, D.C., and is considered Michigan's most important historic building. The **architecture** and design won many awards for **architect** Elijah E. Myers. However, after 100 years of wear and tear, the building needed to be **renovated.** In 1987, the Michigan **legislature** voted to have the building restored to its original state. The current building was completed in 1992.

In 2002, the people of Michigan elected the first female governor in the state's history. Jennifer Granholm served as Michigan's **attorney general** for four years before taking her post as the leader of the state.

Over 125,000 visitors from every state in the nation and many countries around the world tour Michigan's capitol building every year.

Executive Branch

Governor
(four-year term)

Carries out the laws
of the state

Legislative Branch

Michigan General Assembly

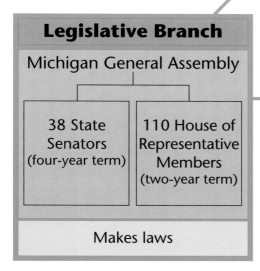

| 38 State Senators (four-year term) | 110 House of Representative Members (two-year term) |

Makes laws

Judicial Branch

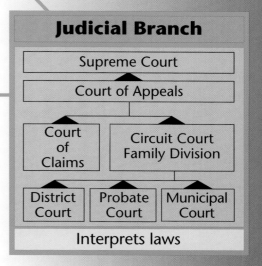

Supreme Court

Court of Appeals

Court of Claims

Circuit Court Family Division

District Court | Probate Court | Municipal Court

Interprets laws

Michigan's state government serves the more than 9,990,000 residents that live in the state.

The Governor's Summer Home

One of the best things about being the governor of Michigan is access to a mansion on Mackinac Island. The governor's summer mansion was purchased in 1945 and has been available to all of Michigan's governors since then. It has 24 rooms, including 11 bedrooms and 8 bathrooms. It also has views of the Mackinac Bridge and the Straits of Mackinac.

National Parks and Natural Areas

Michigan is a great place to be outdoors. The state has more than 3,200 miles of shoreline, 11,000 **inland** lakes, 5,600 miles of snowmobile trails, dozens of downhill ski resorts, and four national parks.

ISLE ROYALE NATIONAL PARK

Isle Royale National Park is located in the northwest corner of Lake Superior, near Wisconsin. It is 45 miles

Isle Royale is the only national park that closes down in the winter. This is because the island has no roads. It can only be reached by boat or float plane.

long and 9 miles wide at its widest point. It is the largest island in Lake Superior. The island has a total area of 850 square miles, including land below water that extends four and a half miles out into Lake Superior. Isle Royale is one of the least visited state parks. Most of the land is wilderness—home to moose, wolves, and more than 200 species of birds.

KEWEENAW NATIONAL HISTORIC PARK

Copper played an important role in Michigan's history. The Keweenaw Peninsula copper mines helped the **industrial** development of the United States. The Keweenaw National Historical Park was established in honor of the rich history of copper mining in the state. The park is about 1,700 acres, but much of it is privately owned and not open to public use.

The cliffs at Pictured Rocks National Lakeshore are made of Cambrian sandstone that is about 500 million years old.

PICTURED ROCKS NATIONAL LAKESHORE

In 1966, Pictured Rocks became the first national lakeshore. Its more than 73,000 acres include cliffs, beaches, sand dunes, waterfalls, inland lakes, wildlife, and forest. It is only five miles wide at its widest point, but it runs along the southern shoreline of Lake Superior for forty miles. The name Pictured Rocks comes from the shapes that appear on the rocks due to the multicolored sandstone and mineral stains.

Sleeping Bear Dunes are not just fun during the summer. There are over 40 miles of marked ski trails for people who enjoy winter sports.

SLEEPING BEAR DUNES NATIONAL LAKESHORE

Sleeping Bear Dunes National Lakeshore covers a 35-mile stretch of Lake Michigan's eastern coastline, as well as North and South Manitou Islands. The park was established because of its natural features, including forests, beaches, dune formations, and other formations created by **glaciers.** The Sleeping Bear Dunes also feature an 1871 lighthouse, three former Life-Saving Service/Coast Guard Stations, and a **rural** historic farm **district.** The dune climb is the most popular in Michigan, with an estimated 300,000 people making the climb every year.

Two Parts, One State

Michigan is the only state that is divided into two distinct parts, both of which are attached to another state. It was not until 1957, when the Mackinac Bridge was built, that the two parts of the state were connected as one.

Businesses and Products

Michigan is a hard-working state. Many people work in the state's factories and laboratories, and on farms. Michigan leads the nation in automobile manufacturing, and is a leader in chemical production and clockmaking. West Michigan plays a large role in the production of office furniture worldwide. Michigan is also home to several food products that are popular around the world.

AUTOMOBILES

Michigan has been home to automobile manufacturers since the **industry** first developed. Today, three companies have their headquarters in the state. General Motors is in Detroit, Ford Motor Company is in Dearborn, and DaimlerChrysler is in Auburn Hills. All three companies have plants in Michigan, across the United States, and around the world. General Motors is one of the largest companies of any kind in the world, and employs the most people in Michigan. Nearly half of all manufacturing jobs in Michigan are related to the auto industry. Companies that make car parts are also located in Michigan.

Many people in Dearborn are Ford Motor Company employees. The company employs nearly 350,000 people worldwide.

CHEMICALS

When he was a young man, Herbert Dow was sometimes dangerous to be around. He was very knowledgeable about chemicals, but accidents led to explosions while trying to make new products. In 1897, he founded the Dow Chemical Company in Midland. Dow was named to the National Inventors' Hall of Fame in 1983. Today, Dow Chemical Company is the world leader in chemicals and employs over 50,000 people around the world.

FURNITURE

Steelcase, Inc. was established in Grand Rapids in 1912. The company has grown to 16,000 employees worldwide. Steelcase helps bring together **architecture,** technology, and furniture to create workspaces that meet the needs of its **clients.**

Herman Miller, of Zeeland, began manufacturing home furniture in 1923. Through the years, his company has been a leader in developing new styles of office furniture. Today, the Herman Miller company sells over $2 billion in products worldwide every year. In 2002, Herman Miller was named *Fortune* magazine's Most Admired Furniture Company for the fifteenth time in sixteen years.

Haworth, Incorporated began as a small manufacturer of custom wood products in 1948. Today it is the second-largest designer and

Furniture for offices and homes are just some of the products Herman Miller produces.

manufacturer of office furniture in the world. In 1993, Haworth was named one of "The 100 Best Companies to Work for in America." Their **corporate** headquarters are in Holland, Michigan.

Grandfather clocks like the one shown here are the specialty of the Howard Miller Clock Company.

CLOCK MANUFACTURERS

Zeeland is also home to several clock manufacturers. Colonial Manufacturing Company was founded in 1906 and was best known for fine wooden cases that held West German clocks. The company was purchased in 1987 and no longer has manufacturing facilities in Zeeland. Sligh Furniture Company has been making clocks in Zeeland since the 1940s. Today, Sligh sells both furniture and clocks. The Howard Miller Clock Company was founded in 1926 and is still run by members of the Howard Miller family. The product line of the Howard Miller Clock Company has been expanded in recent years, but the company is still mostly known worldwide for its beautiful clocks.

BREAKFAST CEREAL

Will K. Kellogg was hired by his brother, Dr. John Harvey Kellogg, to be the business manager of the Battle Creek **Sanitarium.** The sanitarium promoted a healthy lifestyle by not allowing its patients to use caffeine, alcohol, or tobacco, or to eat meat. In 1894, Will Kellogg was testing a wheat bread recipe to serve the patients. While doing so, a batch of boiled grain was forgotten

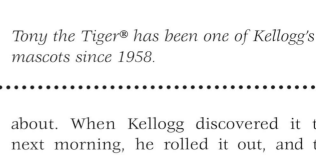

Tony the Tiger® has been one of Kellogg's mascots since 1958.

about. When Kellogg discovered it the next morning, he rolled it out, and the grain came off in little flakes. He baked the flakes and served them with milk. The patients loved them, and cereal was born. By 1902, about 40 cereal companies were open in Battle Creek. Kellogg created the Battle Creek Toasted Corn Flake Company in 1906. It became the Kellogg Company in 1922. Today, Battle Creek is still known as Cereal City.

BABY FOOD

Gerber baby food was created by a frustrated father who got tired of watching his wife strain vegetables to make food for their daughter. Dan Gerber of Fremont began making baby food at the family's **cannery,** testing his creation on his child and other babies of Fremont. Gerber ran an advertisement in magazines to **recruit** other parents to try his product for their children. He offered six cans of baby food for $1.00 if the parents would write the name of their grocery store on the order form. Gerber used this information to convince grocery stores that people wanted his product. At 15 cents per can, Gerber sold 590,000 cans in his first year of business. Today, Gerber offers almost 190 food products that are sold in 80 countries.

The Gerber baby, Ann Turner Cook, has been on the company's products since 1931.

22

Food

The food of Michigan reflects its **agricultural** history. Michigan is a leading producer of several crops, including fruit, beans, and celery. Michigan residents also enjoy several recipes that were brought to the state when their **ancestors immigrated** from European countries.

PASTIES

The pasty (pronounced PAST-ee) most likely originated in Cornwall, England. This food was brought to the Upper Peninsula of Michigan by **immigrants** who worked in the copper and iron mines of the Upper Peninsula. The pasty is **traditionally** made with meat, potatoes, and vegetables layered inside a pastry crust. The triangle-shaped pasty made a complete meal and could be eaten without silverware—even with dirty fingers. The eater would simply throw away the dirty corner he had held. Although the mines closed long ago, the pasty is still an Upper Peninsula specialty that has found its way into homes throughout the state.

Some people say pasties are like pizza—everyone has their favorite type. Ketchup and gravy are popular pasty toppings.

Mackinac Island Fudge

Always have an adult help you in the kitchen.

1/2 cup milk

1/2 cup butter

1/2 cup brown sugar

1/2 cup granulated sugar

1/8 teaspoon salt

1 teaspoon vanilla extract

2 cups confectioners' sugar

1/2 cup cocoa

1/2 cup nuts (optional)

Mix milk, butter, brown sugar, granulated sugar, and salt in heavy pan. Cook at medium heat until boiling. Boil for exactly 6 minutes, stirring constantly. Remove from heat and add vanilla extract, cocoa, and confectioners' sugar. Beat with a mixer until smooth and thick. Add nuts, if desired. Pour the mixture into a buttered pan and freeze for 20 minutes. Cut into pieces. Makes approximately one pound of fudge.

FUDGE

Mackinac Island fudge was first made in 1887. The **industry** was started by a man named Newton Jerome Murdick who loved his mother's fudge recipe. He thought visitors to the island would enjoy it too, so he began making fudge and selling it. The fudge became so popular that other people on the island opened their own fudge stores, too! Residents of the Upper Peninsula have nicknamed tourists to their area fudgies because visitors can always be found in the fudge shops, buying sweets to take back home.

FRUIT

The **climate** along Lake Michigan provides the perfect conditions for growing fruit. In fact, the western edge of the Lower Peninsula is called the fruit belt. Several types of fruit, including cherries, blueberries, and apples, are grown in this area.

Michigan is the biggest producer of tart cherries in the United States. Michigan produces over 250 million pounds of cherries each year! About 75 percent of the tart cherries eaten in the United States are grown in Michigan. Tart cherries are usually canned or frozen to be used in pies and other baked goods. The state also produces about 15 to 20 percent of the nation's sweet cherries.

Michigan is also the leading producer of blueberries in the United States. In recent years, the state has produced around 49 million pounds of the berries each year. Allegan, Berrien, Muskegon, Ottawa, and Van Buren counties on the western side of Michigan's Lower Peninsula are the state's primary blueberry growing region. Blueberries in Michigan are ready to be picked from mid-July to late September.

According to the Guinness Book of World Records, *the largest apple ever picked came from Caro, Michigan. It weighed three pounds, two ounces!*

Michigan is ranked third in the country for growing apples. About one billion pounds of apples are grown each year. There are many apple orchards and cider mills in the state that offer the opportunity for people to pick their own apples.

MAPLE SYRUP

In the Thumb area of Michigan, near Saginaw, farmers grow crops of sugar beets. These beets are used to produce sugar. Maple syrup is made of this sugar and the sap of maple trees. Michigan is one of the leading states in maple syrup production.

BEANS

Michigan grows more dry beans than any other state. Michigan's climate and soil make the state an excellent place to grow this crop. Almost half of 295,000 acres of beans grown in the state are navy beans. Michigan also produces black, cranberry, kidney, pinto, and other dry beans. More than 1,500 pounds of beans are harvested each year. About 90 percent of Michigan beans are canned. Many beans are **exported** to Europe and other countries.

CELERY

Farmers in the Kalamazoo area were the first to grow celery in the United States. The seeds were brought to the area in the 1850s from Scotland. Dutch farmers living in the Kalamazoo area had the knowledge and skills necessary to use the available soil to grow the crop. Today, Michigan ranks second in the United States in celery production.

Although Michigan's celery-growing season is only four months long, the state is one of the leading producers of the vegetable.

DAIRY

The dairy business brings in the most money of all of Michigan's farm businesses. About 300,000 milk cows in Michigan produce 712,500,000 gallons of milk each year. The average milk cow in Michigan produces over 19,000 pounds of milk a year all by herself! These hard-working cows make Michigan the eighth-ranked milk-producing state in the nation.

The milk is also used to make other dairy products such as butter, yogurt, sour cream, cream cheese, and ice cream.

Michigan is home to approximately 52,000 farms. They cover 10.4 million acres of the state.

Sports

Michigan sports fans have a wide variety of teams to support and cheer on. Detroit is home to several professional teams, and there are many college, semi-professional, and minor league teams across the state as well.

DETROIT LIONS

The Detroit Lions have been a Michigan sports **tradition** for many years. The original football team played in Portsmouth, Ohio, and was called the Spartans, but in 1934 the team was purchased for just under $8,000 and moved to Detroit. The Lions had much success in their early years in the National Football League (NFL), winning the national championship in 1935. The Lions dominated the NFL in the 1950s with four division titles and three league championships. The team won back-to-

Barry Sanders was a star running back for the Detroit Lions. He holds 16 team rushing records.

A Thanksgiving Tradition

Every year since 1934, except during World War II, the Detroit Lions have played a game on Thanksgiving Day. The tradition was started when the Detroit Lions' owner, G. A. Richards, was trying to boost attendance at the games. Midwestern high schools had a tradition of playing football games on Thanksgiving Day that were well-attended, so Richards decided to invite the Chicago Bears to Detroit to play that day as well. The idea worked. Over 26,000 people showed up for the game, and many more were turned away because there were no seats left.

back championships in 1952 and 1953, and earned its last title in 1957. Since then, the Lions have experienced both successful and unsuccessful seasons. They were National Football Conference (NFC) Central Division champions in 1983, 1991, and 1993. Many talented players have been members of the Detroit Lions, and twelve of them are in the NFL Hall of Fame.

DETROIT TIGERS

The Tigers professional baseball team has been a part of Detroit for over 100 years. In 1901, they took the field in Bennett Park. Tiger Stadium, at the corner of Michigan and Trumbull Avenues in Detroit, was the team's home until 1999, when Comerica Park opened for the 2000 season. The Tigers have been world champions four times—1935, 1945, 1968, and 1984—and have nineteen

Ty Cobb

Ty Cobb is considered one of the best players in baseball history. He played for the Detroit Tigers for twenty-two years and was their manager for six years. He was named to the Baseball Hall of Fame in 1936. Cobb was responsible for the first-ever professional baseball strike. A **spectator** was **taunting** Cobb from the stands, and Cobb got into a fight with him. Cobb was suspended from baseball, and his teammates refused to play unless the suspension was lifted. When it was not, the Tigers did not play their next game, and each player was fined $100. Cobb told his team to return to the field. He paid a $50 fine and sat out for ten games.

players in the National Baseball Hall of Fame.

DETROIT PISTONS

Fred Zollner launched the Fort Wayne Zollner Pistons, a professional basketball team, in 1941. He named the team after himself and his company's product, automobile pistons. The team became the Detroit Pistons in 1957. The Pistons were National Basketball Association (NBA) world champions during the 1988–1989 and 1989–1990 seasons.

DETROIT RED WINGS

The Detroit Red Wings have brought much excitement to Michigan hockey fans in recent years, winning the Stanley Cup title in 1997, 1998, and 2002. However, these were not the first championships in the team's history. They were also champions in 1936, 1937, 1943, 1950, 1952, 1954, and 1955. The team was established in 1926 as the Detroit Cougars. Their name changed to the Detroit Red Wings in 1932.

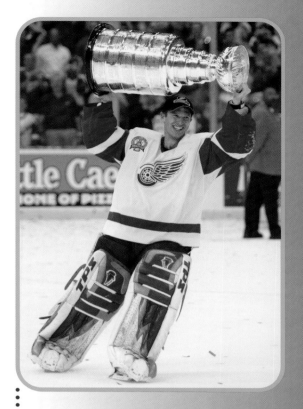

Detroit Red Wings goalie Dominik Hasek skates with the Stanley Cup after the team's victory on June 13, 2002.

DETROIT SHOCK

The Women's National Basketball League (WNBA) was formed in 1996. The Detroit Shock joined the league in 1998. The team has played hard during the first few years in the league, and has a bright future in representing Detroit across the country.

In 2003, the Detroit Shock went from the last place team in the league to league champions in just one season.

Minor League Baseball

Michigan is home to three minor league baseball teams: the Lansing Lugnuts, the West Michigan Whitecaps, and the Michigan Battle Cats. All three teams play "A" level baseball, preparing the players to move up into the major leagues. The Lugnuts are part of the Chicago Cubs, the Whitecaps are part of the Detroit Tigers, and the Battle Cats, also called the Battle Creek Yankees, are with the New York Yankees.

Women's Baseball

When men went off to war during World War II (1939–1945), Philip K. Wrigley created the All American Girls Professional Baseball League in 1943. Michigan had five teams: the Grand Rapids Chicks, the Muskegon Lassies, the Muskegon Belles, the Kalamazoo Lassies, and the Battle Creek Belles. The league ended play in 1954. Today, the Detroit Danger women's semi-professional baseball team plays in the Great Lakes Women's Baseball League.

The women's baseball teams during WWII had fifteen players, a coach, a business manager, and a female chaperone. Their rules were similar to men's baseball.

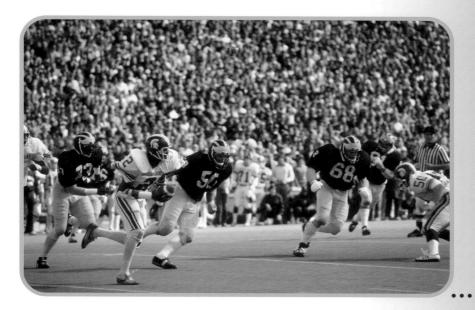

The yearly football game between the University of Michigan and Michigan State is always exciting to watch.

COLLEGE SPORTS

Michigan is home to over 60 four-year universities and colleges, many of which have excellent sports programs. Two of the biggest athletic programs include those at Michigan State University (MSU) and the University of Michigan (U-M). Both schools are part of the Big Ten college conference. In recent years, MSU has excelled in men's basketball and men's hockey. U-M has succeeded in men's football, men's gymnastics, and men's hockey. The **rivalry** between U-M and MSU is one of the most competitive in the nation.

Unusual Football Trophies

The MSU Spartan football team competes for four different "trophies" each year. The Paul Bunyon Governor's Trophy goes to the winner of the MSU versus U-M game. The Old Brass **Spittoon** goes to the winner of the MSU versus Indiana University game. The Megaphone Trophy is the prize for the winner of the MSU versus Notre Dame game, and the Land Grant trophy goes to the winner of the game between MSU and the Nittany Lions of Penn State.

The University of Michigan football team also competes for more than just a win. The Little Brown Jug is given to the winner of the U-M versus Minnesota game.

Attractions and Landmarks

Travel and **tourism** are two of Michigan's biggest **industries.** Each year, millions of people travel to the state. Besides all the natural **resources** in the state, there are many **cultural** and historical sites to visit as well.

Michigan Things to See

Marquette Underwater Preserve

Soo Locks

Grand Hotel

Bottle Cap Museum

Cherry Capital of the World

Bottle House Historical Museum

S.S. City of Milwaukee

Ludington Car Ferry

Sanilac Petroglyphs

World's Largest Weather Vane

Great Lakes Naval Memorial and Museum

Frederik Meijer Gardens and Sculpture Park

Flint

Grand Haven Musical Fountain

Grand Rapids

Windmill Island

Lansing

Saugatuck Chain Ferry

Cereal City

Kalamazoo Air Zoo

Ann Arbor

Detroit

Cabela's

N W E S

0   100 mi

SE Mic

Saginaw

Bronner's Christmas Wonderlan

Flint

Michigan State University Children's Gardens

East Lansing

Lansing

Michigan Historical Museum

Michigan Transit Museum

Renaissance Ce

Detroit

Ann Arbor Hands-On Museum

The Henry Ford

Ann Arbor

MACKINAC BRIDGE

When Michigan became a state, its two **peninsulas** were not connected. The closest point between the peninsulas is the Straits of Mackinac, which is approximately four miles long. Because of the distance and difficulty to get back and forth, people wanted to improve transportation and **commerce.** In 1923, the State Highway Department started ferry service across the Straits. The ferryboats were very popular and the demand increased. In the last year of operation, the ferries transported 900,000 vehicles, but they could not keep up with the demand. Something else had to be done, and the idea of building a bridge began.

For people who are scared to drive over the Mackinac Bridge, there is a service called the "Drivers Assistance Program" that will get them across.

After many attempts, the bridge construction started in 1954. About 3,500 construction workers took part in building the bridge. It turned out to be a dangerous job, as five men lost their lives during the project. The five-mile bridge was completed in 1957.

Today, the Mackinac Bridge is an important link between the two peninsulas. Nearly two million vehicles cross the bridge each year.

Labor Day Walk

Labor Day is the only day of the year when people are allowed to walk across the Mackinac Bridge. More than 70,000 people walk across the bridge that day, including the current governor of Michigan. President George H. W. Bush participated in the walk in 1992.

A tour boat gives visitors an up-close look at the Soo Locks as well as provides some history of the area.

Soo Locks

The St. Mary's River is the only connection between Lake Superior and the other Great Lakes. In a section of the river known as the St. Mary's Rapids, the water falls about twenty-one feet from the level of Lake Superior to the level of the lower lakes. Because of this, boats could not safely **navigate** the river. Early settlers and Native Americans had to unload their boats, haul the cargo around the rapids in wagons, and reload in other boats. In 1797, the first set of locks, called the Sault Ste. Marie Locks, or Soo Locks for short, was built to allow boats to pass through the rapids. These locks were destroyed during the War of 1812, and boats had to be **portaged** around the rapids once again. In May of 1855, a new set of locks was completed. The locks provided an important **commerce** route, and soon there was a need for larger locks to accommodate more ships. In 1881, control of the locks was given to the U.S. government, which built the locks that still stand today.

Today, the Soo Locks are the largest waterway traffic system on Earth. There are four sets of locks that are in continuous use by both ships and **recreational** boats. Approximately 5,000 boats use the locks yearly.

FREDERIK MEIJER GARDENS AND SCULPTURE PARK

Frederik Meijer is probably best known for his Meijer stores that began in Grand Rapids, but Meijer also dreamed of having a **botanical** garden. In 1995, the Frederik Meijer Gardens and Sculpture Park was opened in Grand Rapids. This 125-acre park has more than just flowers. It has the largest tropical **conservatory** in Michigan, **premier** sculpture galleries and exhibits of sculptures by famous artists, indoor specialty gardens, and outdoor gardens with nature

Il Cavallo *is the one of the largest bronze sculptures of a horse in the world. It was created by Nina Akamu, based on drawings done by Leonardo da Vinci.*

trails, a boardwalk, and sculpture pathways. In 1999, a three-story high horse sculpture by Leonardo da Vinci was added to the collection as well.

THE HENRY FORD

Henry Ford wanted to create a learning place where Americans could learn how their **ancestors** lived and worked in the late 1800s and early 1900s. Ford began to fill his eight-acre building in Dearborn with items that would one day be priceless. When this building opened in 1933, it was called The Edison Institute. Today, The Henry Ford is made up of a museum, a historic village, an IMAX theater, a research center, and a factory.

Some say that Ford set out to buy "one of everything made in America" from the late 1800s and early 1900s. The Henry Ford Museum houses one of the largest collections of its kind. In addition to an amazing collection of historic automobiles, the museum also has a huge display of bicycles, plows, canning jars, saw mills, electric fans, steam engines, rocking chairs, early airplanes, and other items. Over the years, the staff has continued to add items to the museum that reflect America's past.

Ford also collected buildings and brought them together on ninety acres of land next to the museum. Today's Greenfield Village consists of over eighty historic structures that were built in different parts of the United States at different time periods. It provides life-size snapshots of American **architecture** and **industry.** In Greenfield Village, Thomas Edison's laboratory from New Jersey is only a few yards from the shop where the Wright brothers built their first airplane in Dayton, Ohio.

The Henry Ford hosts over 1.6 million visitors each year. It is the largest museum in the United States that has exhibits both indoors and outside.

Unusual Exhibit

When Henry Ford learned that his good friend Thomas Edison was dying, Ford asked Edison's son to collect one of his father's last exhaled breaths. Edison's son did so, and the sealed **vial** is on display at the Henry Ford Museum.

CABELA'S

Cabela's, a store for outdoor **recreation** needs in Dundee, is unlike any other store. Cabela's is not only a store, but also an educational center and museum. Visitors are first greeted by the world's largest bronze wildlife sculpture of two 20-foot tall fighting grizzly bears. The store also has 65,000-gallon tanks filled with a variety of freshwater fish **native** to Michigan and the Northeast. The 40-foot Conservation Mountain, complete with running waterfalls, is called "Animals of North America." It features approximately 100 wild game **mounts** in their distinct **habitats,** from a western **prairie** and Michigan woodland to the Alaskan **tundra** and arctic ice. In 2002, Cabela's was Michigan's top tourist destination, with over 6.1 million people visiting the store.

Bronner's carries many unique Christmas items in its large store.

BRONNER'S CHRISTMAS WONDERLAND

The first of Wally Bronner's stores opened in 1954. Since then, Bronner's in Frankenmuth has been a popular destination for people from all over the country and the world, with over 2 million visitors each year. Bronner's Christmas Wonderland is the largest Christmas store in the United States, both in size and the number of items it carries. The store has over 50,000 gifts and other Christmas items in stock, and the Wonderland itself covers 27 acres.

SAUGATUCK CHAIN FERRY

In Saugatuck, a hand-cranked chain ferry brings passengers 225 feet across the Kalamazoo River. Built in 1838, the ferry is the only one of its kind still in operation in the United States.

Many visitors to Saugatuck take a ride on the chain ferry to see both sides of the town.

Folklore and Legends

Folklore and legends are stories that people tell over and over again. These stories often get passed down from older family members to younger ones. The stories may not always be completely true, but they usually have some parts that are based on fact.

SINGAPORE

Along the Kalamazoo River near Lake Michigan lies the site of a "lost city" once known as Singapore. Early in the 1800s, Singapore was a sawmill town. It was founded in 1836 by Horace Comstock as a trading post for settlers who were coming to Michigan. This trading post grew into a town with a bank, sawmills, boarding houses, hotels, general stores, and a lighthouse. However, it was not very long before the timber was gone and the last sawmill was moved further north where the forests still grew thick. The people of Singapore left the town to find jobs. As the town was **abandoned,** the sand dunes shifted, burying the town under the sand. The last family left Singapore around 1890 after the first floor of their house filled with sand. By the 1920s, Singapore was completely buried.

A sign telling the story of Singapore stands next to Saugatuck Village Hall.

Today, the site where Singapore once stood is still covered in sand, but the buildings are no longer there. At least ten homes and parts of others were moved to the town of Saugatuck, four miles from where Singapore stood.

THE LEGEND OF SLEEPING BEAR

The dunes of Sleeping Bear Dunes National Lakeshore and the North and South Manitou Islands are connected by one of Michigan's most famous legends: The Legend of Sleeping Bear.

A Version of The Legend of Sleeping Bear

Long ago along the Wisconsin shoreline, a mother bear and her two cubs were driven into Michigan by a forest fire. The bears swam for many hours, but eventually the cubs grew tired and fell behind. The mother bear reached the shore and climbed to the top of a high bluff to watch and wait for her cubs. The cubs were too tired to keep swimming, and drowned before they reached shore. The mother stayed in her waiting spot, watching for her cubs, until the day she died. The Great Spirit Manitou created two islands to mark the spot where the cubs disappeared and then created a dune to represent the faithful mother bear.

Buildings and Structures

Throughout the state of Michigan, there are many buildings and structures that are unique. Each one adds a piece of history to the state.

SHIPWRECKS

The Great Lakes have provided a means of transportation for hundreds of years. Thousands of boats, from canoes to car ferries and steamers to modern cargo boats, have sailed these large lakes. Approximately 6,000 vessels were lost on the Great Lakes with about 2,000 of these ships located in Michigan waters. Whitefish Point in the Upper Peninsula is at the end of an 80-mile stretch of water that some call the Graveyard of the Great Lakes. Storms coming from the northeast go across 200 miles of open water before reaching this point. This allows the storms to develop a lot of power. These storms have caused over 300 shipwrecks in this area of water alone. The most recent ship lost here was the *Edmund Fitzgerald* in 1976.

LIGHTHOUSES

Michigan is home to 116 lighthouses. Almost all of them have historical or **architectural** significance. Lake Michigan is the only lake of the four surrounding the state with lighthouses that are painted red. Some believe this might be a way to remind tired sailors that they are sailing in Lake Michigan.

The first lighthouse in Michigan was built between 1818 and 1822. The oldest surviving lighthouse is located on

Members of the Coast Guard are stationed at Fort Gratiot's lighthouse and occupy the keeper's house. The lighthouse watches over one of the busiest waterways in the world.

• •

Lake Huron at Fort Gratiot. It was built in 1825. Today, many of the lighthouses are no longer used for **navigation.** However, Michigan is the only state that **preserves** its retired lighthouses. Several organizations in the state work to keep the lighthouses in good condition.

MICHIGAN STATE UNIVERSITY

In 1855, the Michigan **legislature** passed a law that provided for the establishment of the **Agricultural** College of the State of Michigan. The school was opened on May 13, 1857, at what is now East Lansing, the site of the present Michigan State University. Michigan State University was the first agricultural college in the nation. The original **campus** in East Lansing was 677 acres. As additional land was purchased, the campus and farms has grown to cover almost 5,200 acres.

DE ZWAAN WINDMILL

Many residents of Holland, Michigan, can trace their family roots back to the Netherlands. This **heritage** is demonstrated with tulips, wooden shoe factories, and the May Tulip Time festival. Windmill Island, home to De Zwaan Windmill, is also located in Holland.

In order to get the windmill from the Netherlands, Holland had to agree to keep De Zwaan open to the public and continue to use it for grinding flour.

In the early 1960s, a resident named Willard C. Wichers encouraged the Holland City Council to buy a windmill. Wichers located and set up the sale of De Zwaan, a mill in the Netherlands. The windmill was shipped in pieces and arrived in Port Muskegon in October 1964. It was reassembled between 1964 and 1965 on its current site on Windmill Island. De Zwaan was the last windmill to leave the Netherlands. Dutch law now does not allow the sale of windmills, which are treated as national **monuments.**

Today, the De Zwaan windmill still has 80 percent of its original parts. The windmill stands 6-stories tall and weighs around 70 tons. Its blades are 40 feet long and weigh 3 tons each. But despite all that weight, it only takes 15- to 20-mile-per-hour winds to set the blades in motion to grind flour. De Zwaan is the last **authentic** working Dutch windmill in the United States.

GRAND HAVEN MUSICAL FOUNTAIN

In Grand Haven, a large musical fountain entertains visitors by playing music in time to the spraying water. Four billion miles of tape would be needed to record all the musical combinations the fountain can play. The sound system uses 35,000 watts of power—the average home stereo uses only 50. About 20,000 feet of electrical wiring and 40,000 gallons of water keep the fountain running. The fountain plays a nightly show from Memorial Day to Labor Day.

Nightly shows by the fountain last 20 to 25 minutes. It takes an hour to program a single minute of each show!

THE BOTTLE HOUSE

In 1941 John J. Makinen Sr. built a house in Kalkeva that was made entirely from soft-drink bottles. Most of the 60,000 bottles came from the Northwest Bottle Company, where Makinen worked. The house still stands today, and is used as the Kalkeva Historical Society.

RENAISSANCE CENTER

The Renaissance Center in Detroit was constructed during the late 1970s and opened in 1981. Henry Ford II wanted to help bring the city of Detroit out of the **ruins** by building a spectacular hotel and convention center. The Renaissance Center has four 39-story office towers that surround the 73-story, 1,298-room Marriott Detroit Renaissance Center hotel. In 2002 the hotel underwent a

The Detroit Renaissance Center is the tallest building in Michigan.

Because Mackinac Island does not allow cars, guests of the Grand Hotel arrive and leave by horse-drawn carriage.

$100 million **renovation.** From the Center you can see the city of Windsor, in Canada, across the Detroit River. The Center is so large that it even has its own ZIP code!

GRAND HOTEL

The Grand Hotel on Mackinac Island is the world's largest summer hotel. The hotel has been host to many guests over the years, including U.S. Presidents Truman, Kennedy, Ford, George H. W. Bush, and Clinton. At 660 feet, Grand Hotel's front porch is the world's longest, and is visible as you approach the island from Lake Michigan. The hotel has kept strict clothing guidelines for its guests: after 6:00 P.M., men must wear coats and ties, and women must wear evening dresses.

Map of Michigan

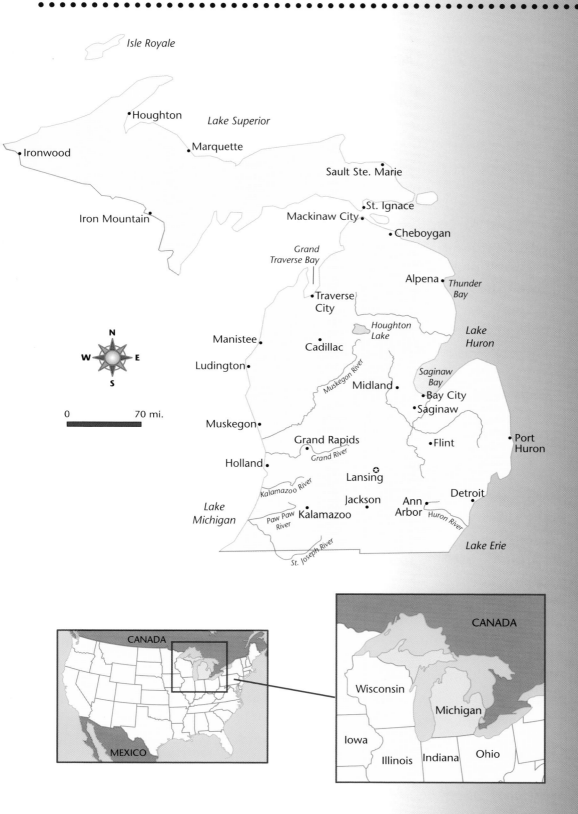

Isle Royale

Lake Superior

•Houghton

•Ironwood

•Marquette

Sault Ste. Marie•

Iron Mountain•

•St. Ignace
Mackinaw City•

•Cheboygan

Grand
Traverse Bay

Alpena• •Thunder
Bay

•Traverse
City

Houghton
Lake

Lake
Huron

Manistee•

Cadillac•

N
W E
S

Ludington•

Muskegon River

Midland•

Saginaw
Bay

•Bay City
•Saginaw

0   70 mi.

Muskegon•

Grand Rapids•

Grand River

•Flint

Port
Huron•

Holland•

Kalamazoo River

✿
Lansing

Lake
Michigan

Paw Paw
River

Kalamazoo•

Jackson•

Ann
Arbor•

Huron River

Detroit•

St. Joseph River

Lake Erie

CANADA

CANADA

MEXICO

Wisconsin

Michigan

Iowa

Illinois   Indiana   Ohio

Glossary

abandoned given up

adopt take as one's own

agricultural having to do with farming

ancestor one from whom an individual has descended

architect person who designs buildings and gives advice on their construction

architecture style of a building

attorney general chief law officer of a nation or state

authentic being what it really seems to be

botanical related to plants

burrow hole in the ground made by an animal for shelter

campaign series of activities meant to get a certain thing done

campus grounds of a university or other school

cannery factory where foods are canned

capital location of a government

capitol building in which the legislature meets

chandelier lighting fixture with several branches that hangs from a ceiling

client person who uses the professional services of another

climate weather conditions that are usual for a certain area

coat of arms heraldic arms belonging to a person, family, or a group or a representation of these, as on a shield

commerce buying and selling goods

conservatory greenhouse

corporate main offices of a company

cultural related to the ideas, skills, arts, and a way of life of a certain people at a certain time

district area or section set aside for a special purpose

economic of, relating to, or based on the making, buying, and selling of goods

endangered species threatened with extinction

executive branch of government that makes sure the laws of a state or nation are carried out

export sending of goods out of the country

fossil remains of a prehistoric plant or animal that have turned to stone

glacier large sheet of ice that spreads or retreats very slowly over land

habitat place where an animal or plant lives and grows

heritage something that comes from one's ancestors

hibernate to pass through the winter in a resting state

immigrant one who moves to another country to settle

immigrate to move to another country to settle

industry group of businesses that offer a similar product or service

inland not near the coast

interpret make meaning out of

judicial branch of government that includes the courts; the judicial branch explains or interprets the laws of the state or nation

legislative branch of government that makes the laws

legislature governmental body that makes and changes laws. A member of the legislature is a legislator.

lieutenant governor second-in-command of a state, after the governor

lyric words to a song

mastodon prehistoric relative of today's elephant

monument structure meant to keep alive the memory of a person or event

mount display by fastening in position on a support

native originally from a place

navigate to steer or direct the course of

nominate choose as a candidate for

peninsula piece of land that is surrounded by water on three sides

portage carrying boats and goods over land from one body of water to another

prairie large area of grassland

premier first in position and importance

preserve to keep or save from injury or harm

recreation means of refreshing the mind and body

recruit to form or strengthen with new members

renovate to put in good condition again

resource something that is available to take care of a need; there are natural and human-made resources

rivalry competition

ruin complete collapse or destruction

rural having to do with the country or farmland

sanitarium place to go to regain health

spectator person watching an athletic event

spittoon place for spitting

taunting to make fun of or say mean and insulting things to

threatened species group of animals whose numbers are decreasing, bringing the group close to endangerment

tradition custom or belief handed down from generation to generation

tourism relating to traveling for pleasure

tundra treeless plain of arctic regions

vial small container usually made of glass or plastic

More Books to Read

Burcar, Colleen. *Michigan Curiosities: Quirky Characters, Roadside Oddities & Other Offbeat Stuff.* Old Saybrook, Conn.: Globe Pequot Press, 2003.

McAuliffe, Emily. *Michigan Facts and Symbols.* Minnetonka, Minn.: Bridgestone Books, 1999.

Van Frankenhuysen, Gijsbert and Kathy-Jo Wargin. *The Legend of Sleeping Bear.* Chelsea, Mi.: Sleeping Bear Press, 1998.

Index

About the Author

Nichole Thieda is a lifelong summer resident of Michigan. A member of Phi Beta Kappa, she graduated from Michigan State University with a degree in English education. Nichole currently works as an editor and freelance writer. Her writing has appeared in *The Grand Rapids Press*, TECHLearning.com, and *Women's LifeStyle*, a syndicated magazine for women.